Theory Paper   Grade 4   2018   A
Model Answers

1 (4)

(a) **maestoso** means:

movement ☐

in the style of a march ☐

sustained ☐

majestic ✔

cantando means:

dying away ☐

singing ✔

calm ☐

tenderly ☐

(b) true (2)

(c) (2)

or ... / *or* ...

or ... *or* ...

(d) leading note (2)

(e) six (2)

(f) (3)

2 (a)   minor 6th   diminished 5th   major 7th (6)

(b) (4)

3 (a) (10)

or ...

or ...

(b)

4 (a) (i)   X appoggiatura / leaning note   (2)

              Y trill / shake   (2)

    (ii) Bar 4   (2)

    (iii) B flat   (2)

    (iv) E flat   (2)

  (b) (i)   (4)

    (ii) Similarity   rhythm / pitch / slurs / staccatissimo   (1)

           Difference   dynamics   (1)

    (iii) true   (2)

    (iv)   *vite*   (2)

  (c) (i) flute / oboe / clarinet   (2)

    (ii) trumpet   (2)

    (iii) double bass   (2)

    (iv)   timpani   bass drum   (4)

5   (10)

6   (10)

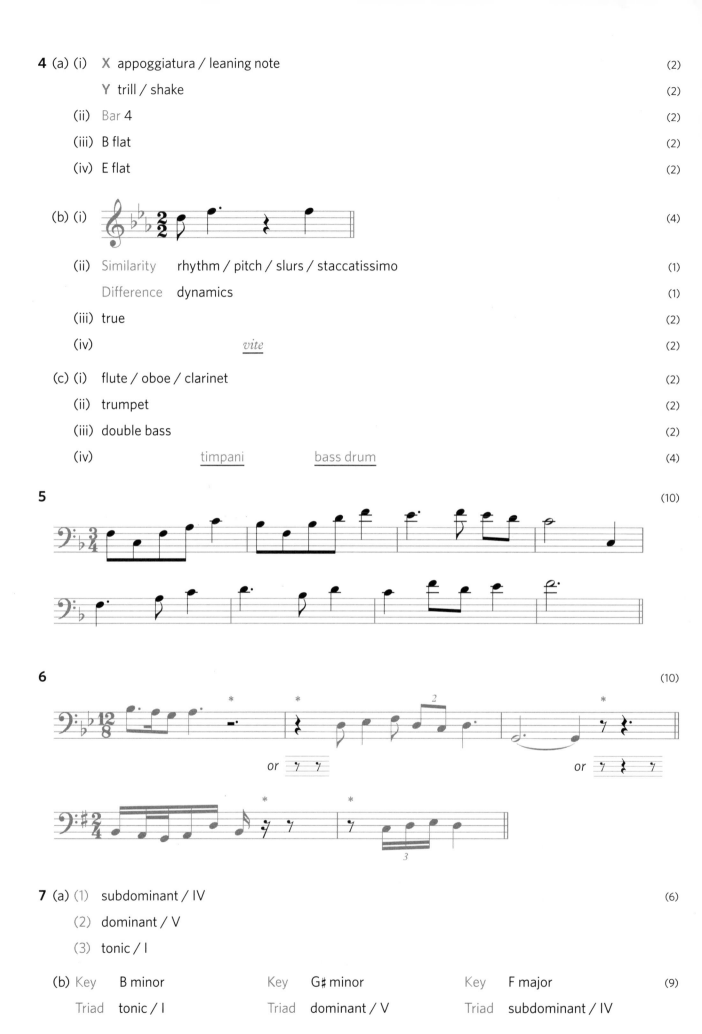

7 (a) (1) subdominant / IV   (6)

    (2) dominant / V

    (3) tonic / I

  (b) Key   B minor   Key   G♯ minor   Key   F major   (9)

    Triad tonic / I   Triad dominant / V   Triad subdominant / IV

Music Theory Practice Papers 2018

Model Answers

ABRSM Grade 4

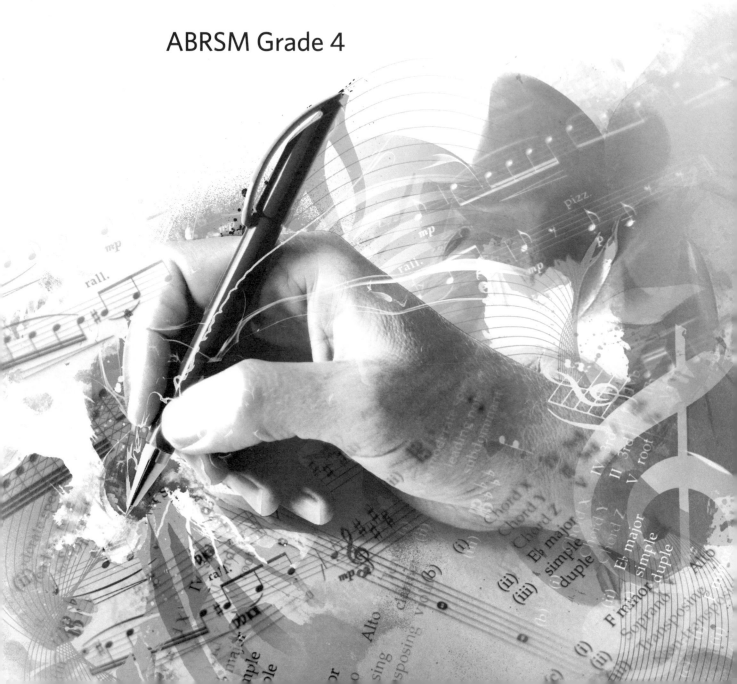

Welcome to ABRSM's *Music Theory Practice Papers 2018 Model Answers*, Grade 4. These answers are a useful resource for students and teachers preparing for ABRSM theory exams and should be used alongside the relevant published theory practice papers.

For more information on how theory papers are marked and some general advice on taking theory exams, please refer to **www.abrsm.org/theory**.

Using these answers

- Answers are given in the same order and, where possible, in the same layout as in the exam papers, making it easy to match answer to question.

- Where it is necessary to show the answer on a stave, the original stave is printed in grey with the answer shown in black, for example:

- Alternative answers are separated by an oblique stroke (/) or by *or*, for example:

    getting slower / gradually getting slower

- The old-style crotchet rest ↯ is accepted as a valid alternative to the modern symbol 𝄽 .

- Answers that require the candidate to write out a scale or chord have been shown at one octave only. Reasonable alternatives at different octaves can also receive full marks.

- Sometimes the clef, key and time signature of the relevant bar(s) are included for added clarity, for example:

© 2019 by The Associated Board of the Royal Schools of Music
Published by ABRSM (Publishing) Ltd, a wholly owned subsidiary of ABRSM
Cover by Kate Benjamin & Andy Potts
Printed in England by Halstan & Co. Ltd, Amersham, Bucks., on materials from sustainable sources
Reprinted in 2019

Theory Paper   Grade 4   2018   B
Model Answers

1   (4)

(a) **Tempo giusto** means: **senza rall.** means:

  with some freedom of time ☐   getting faster ☐

  at the same speed ☐   without getting slower ☑

  in strict time ☑   held back ☐

  first time ☐   slow ☐

(b) acciaccatura / grace note / crushed note   (2)

(c)   (4)

(d) eight   (2)

(e) A   (1)

(f)   (2)

2 (a)   augmented 5th   minor 7th   major 2nd   (6)

  (b)   (4)

3   (10)

  (a)

  (b)

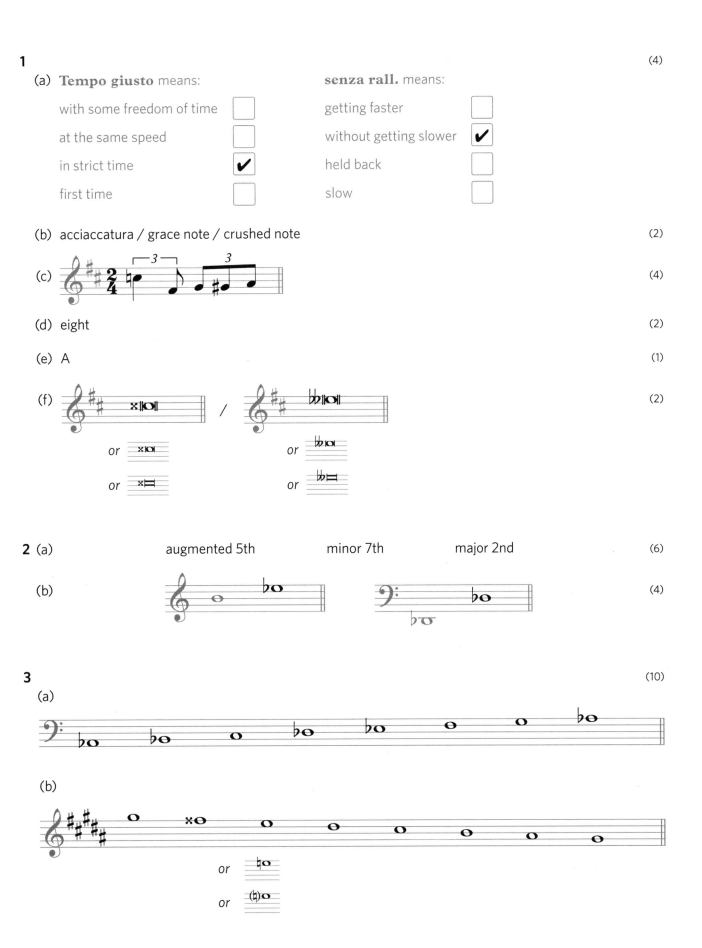

5

4 (a) (i) supertonic (2)

(ii) _très_ (2)

(iii) **Vivace** means: (2)

slow ☐

lively, quick ☑

gradually getting quicker ☐

at a medium speed ☐

(iv) (4)

(b) (i) false (2)

true (2)

(ii) (4)

(iii) Bar 6 (2)

(c) (i) String   violin / viola / harp (2)

Woodwind   flute / oboe / clarinet / cor anglais (2)

(ii) tuba / bass tuba (2)

(iii) Definite pitch   timpani / kettledrums / xylophone / marimba / (2)
glockenspiel / vibraphone / celesta / tubular bells

Indefinite pitch   side drum / snare drum / bass drum / cymbals / (2)
triangle / tambourine / castanets / tam-tam

5 (10)

(a)

(b) compound

duple

6 (10)

(a)

(b)

7 (a) (1)   tonic / I (6)

(2)   subdominant / IV

(3)   dominant / V

(b) (9)

6

Theory Paper   Grade 4   2018   C
Model Answers

1 (4)

(a) **Tempo comodo** means:

slow, stately	☐
first time	☐
at a comfortable speed	✔
in time	☐

morendo means:

dying away	✔
becoming more lively	☐
calm	☐
hurrying	☐

(b)  (3)

(c) two / two crotchets / two quarter notes / one minim / one half note / one beat   (2)

(d) simple   (1)

duple   (1)

(e) false   (2)

(f) G minor   (2)

2 (a)   major 7th   diminished 4th   minor 2nd   (6)

(b)   (4)

3 (10)

(a)

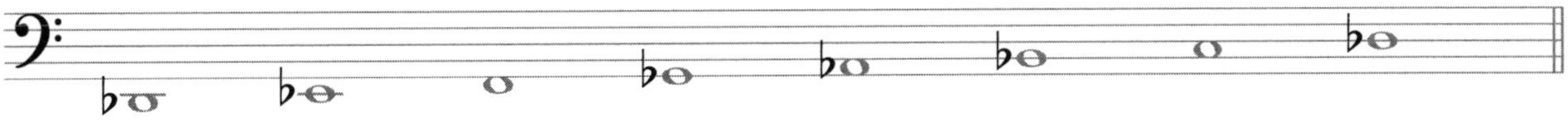

(b)

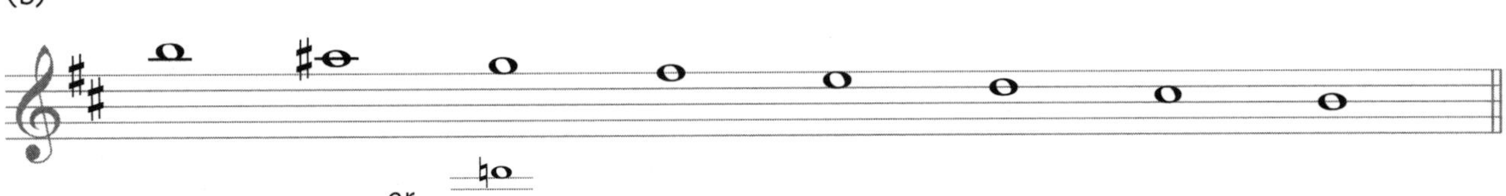

or

or

4 (a) (i)   *lent*   (2)

    (ii) **A** appoggiatura / leaning note   (2)

           B turn / upper turn   (2)

    (iii)   (2)

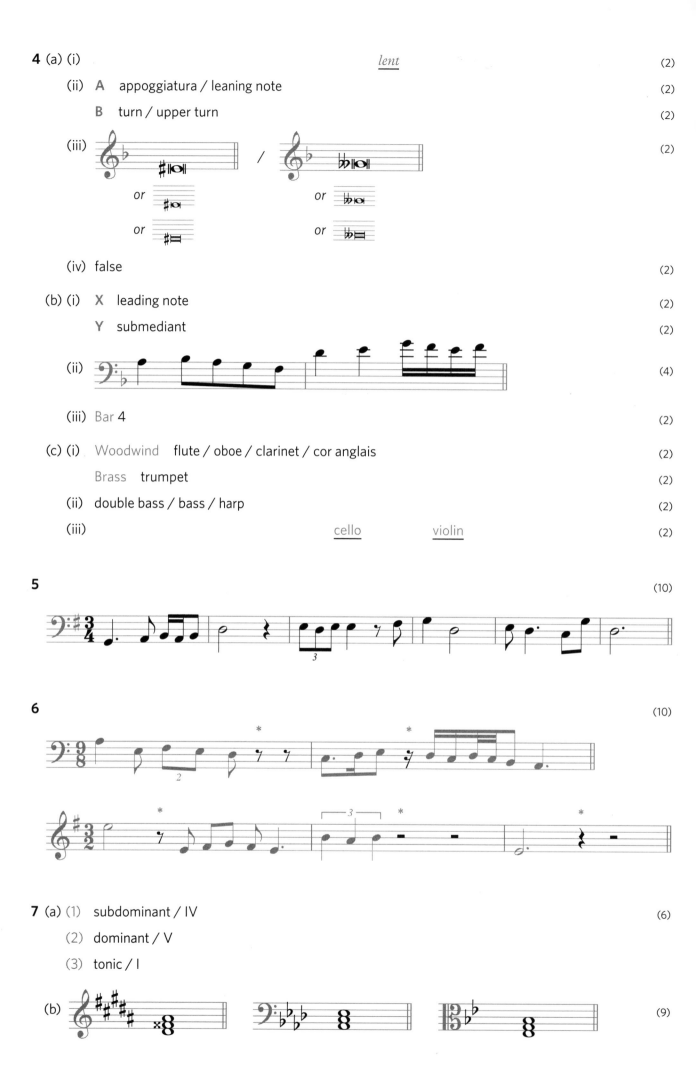

    (iv) false   (2)

(b) (i) **X** leading note   (2)

           Y submediant   (2)

    (ii)   (4)

    (iii) Bar 4   (2)

(c) (i) Woodwind   flute / oboe / clarinet / cor anglais   (2)

            Brass   trumpet   (2)

    (ii) double bass / bass / harp   (2)

    (iii)   cello   violin   (2)

5   (10)

6   (10)

7 (a) (1) subdominant / IV   (6)

    (2) dominant / V

    (3) tonic / I

(b)   (9)

Theory Paper   Grade 4   2018   S
Model Answers

1   (4)

(a)   **Scherzando** means: **stringendo** means:

delicate ☐   gradually getting faster ☑

playful, joking ☑   gradually getting slower ☐

sustained ☐   in a singing style ☐

simple, plain ☐   gradually getting quieter ☐

(b)   acciaccatura / grace note / crushed note   (2)

(c)   (2)

(d)   G   (1)

(e)   (4)

(f)   true   (2)

2 (a)   augmented 2nd   diminished 7th   minor 3rd   (6)

(b)   (4)

3   (10)

(a)

(b)

or

or

4 (a) (i) **X** leading note (2)

Y mediant (2)

(ii) C minor (2)

(iii) Bar **7 / 10** (2)

(iv)  (2)

(b) (i) (4)

(ii) **Allegro** (2)

(iii) two (2)

(iv) true (2)

(c) (i) false (2)

(ii) Highest   trumpet (2)

Lowest   tuba / bass tuba (2)

(iii)   double bass   violin (4)

5 (10)

(a)

(b) compound

duple

6   A flat   F sharp (10)

C double sharp   D flat

G double flat   B sharp

7 (a) (1) subdominant / IV (6)

(2) tonic / I

(3) dominant / V

(b) (9)

10

Music Theory Practice Papers 2018 Model Answers

Model answers for four practice papers, adapted from ABRSM's 2018 Music Theory exams for Grade 4

Key features:

- a list of correct answers where appropriate
- a selection of likely options where the answer can be expressed in a variety of ways
- a single exemplar where a composition-style answer is required

Support material for ABRSM Music Theory exams

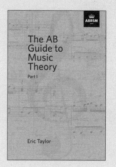

**Supporting the teaching and learning of music
in partnership with the Royal Schools of Music**

Royal Academy of Music | Royal College of Music
Royal Northern College of Music | Royal Conservatoire of Scotland

www.abrsm.org f facebook.com/abrsm
🐦 @abrsm ▶ ABRSM YouTube

ISBN 978-1-78601-206-7

9 781786 012067